Numbers in Our World

Rachel Griffiths and Margaret Clyne

We see numbers on the clock.
What do the numbers tell us?

We see numbers on the sign.
What do the numbers tell us?

5

We see numbers on the door.
What do the numbers tell us?

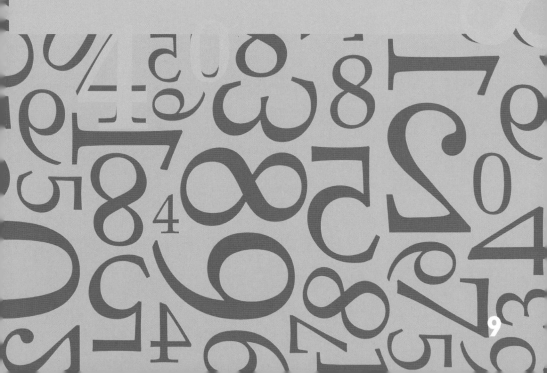

We see numbers on the shirts.
What do the numbers tell us?

We see numbers on
the mailboxes.
What do the numbers tell us?

We see numbers at the market.
What do the numbers tell us?